Alicia Su Lozeron

Introduction

WRITINGS IN THE TIME OF CORONAVIRUS contains a collection of Alicia Su Lozeron's articles about various topics concerning the world during the Covid-19 pandemic. In bringing the human struggles or the hardships and sufferings of the unprecedented time to the forefront, the author emphasizes an empathetic and resilient mindset in achieving peace and growth for our global village. Trials and tribulations may wear the world down, but humanity proves to be strong enough to uphold positive learnings and improvements to be the outcomes of this difficult period.

The articles collected in this book are written with a purpose of raising global awareness about cultural sensitivity and competency, of applying human empathy to a larger context and reach understanding and mutual support among communities, peoples, and nations. They aim to connect the world. By researching and analyzing facts as well as observing societies of cross-cultural nature, Alicia Su Lozeron compels the world to observe and think critically for a more peaceful and prosperous global community, which has been a consistent subject of her writings and works.

Through her work with her publisher/ communication management/travel consulting company, Asia-America Connection Society, AACS 亚美合作协会, Alicia Su Lozeron has been promoting and urging global competence and collaboration. The gentle tolerance or compassion she has been endorsing to attain cultural competence becomes particularly significant in the trying time of a global pandemic. She realizes that her work has just begun and her continual diligence in the advocacy of a meaningful global alliance has proven to be crucial and necessary.

Alicia Su Lozeron writes to seek her own personal fulfillment, and to meet the global village's needs. For herself, the work is her cause and calling. She gains a great deal of gratification through hard work and creation. For the world, her work is beneficial and educational in the ways it studies and portrays peoples and cultures of various heritages and embraces world citizens of the global village – they all deserve to be treated with respect and gain fair access of healthcare and resources, especially during the pandemic.

Alicia Su Lozeron's advocacy for mutual understanding and collaboration among cultures is vital for your community or personal accomplishments, on a business, cultural, educational, or entertainment dimension. Below is what readers and audiences have discerned of Alicia Su Lozeron's work:

• helps me overcome difficulties or fears and find beauty in positive human interactions;

• helps me appreciate people of various backgrounds, and expand knowledge about the world;

• helps me understand interracial or blended family relations;

• helps me savor intricate feelings and emotions about important subjects in life;

• helps me gain enjoyment through poetic narrations;

• helps me realize a new perspective of hope, courage, and respect for others;

• helps me raise awareness about cultural competence;

• helps me nurture a well-rounded global outlook;

• motivates me to promote an open/just community;

• urges me to develop the ability to see the big picture using multiple frames of references;
• helps me strengthen the ability to express genuine love;
• helps me decrease conflict by learning to trust and to resolve disagreements….

"Think Global Live Noble" -- together we can build a better world!

ISBN: 978-1-7332039-3-7

Works by Alicia Su Lozeron --

The Un-death of Me: Life of an Asian American Woman
(2016, A Cross-genre "Fictional Memoir")
Asia-literacy and Global Competence: Collections and Recollections
(2017, English and Chinese Versions)
Global Competence Revisited
(2019, English and Chinese Versions)
Writings in the Time of Coronavirus
(2021, English and Chinese Versions)

Upcoming --

A Man with Immense Love
The Un-death of Me: Life of an Asian American Woman
(Chinese Version; Japanese and Spanish Versions by Teams of Translators)

I dedicate this book not only to all the professionals, friends, colleagues, world citizens and travelers I have come across while exploring the world and acquiring knowledge of it, but also the average citizens who are on the same boat during the testing time of the Covid-19 pandemic. I also thank Robert Alan Lozeron, my dear husband, my love, my life-partner, and my editor who provides me with invaluable suggestions. Those who propel me to reflect on my inner self and the world appear in many facets and aspects of the articles collected in this book. They formulate the pillars of the world as I construct and understand. The factual or fictional world's intricacy lies in their existences. I, in turn, learn and grow constantly while observing and reflecting on the sufferings and joys of the people during the time of the Coronavirus.

With them, this book comes to life.

New York, Las Vegas, Los Angeles, Vancouver,
Toronto, London, Sydney

Asia-America Connection Society

Global Competence Revisited

Writings in the Time of Coronavirus

Alicia Su Lozeron

We must learn from the pandemic experiences -- we must examine the impacts of COVID-19 on globalization and readjust relevant courses: trade, travel, mobility, economy, food, supply chains, resources, jobs, education, entertainment, sports, and healthcare systems -- all aspects of human life. We must take the lessons to heart.

With collaborations at local, state, and federal levels, a holistic approach to fighting racism against Asian Americans may just intervene and correct some aberrant minds.

The ubiquity of digital socialization and communications calls for thorough research on regulatory aspects of digital media use, including their ramifications for politics, journalism, public services, entertainment, gaming, e-commerce, education, healthcare, science or medical communication, and other areas.

-- Alicia Su Lozeron

Content

Introduction

1. Globalization in the Time of Coronavirus
2. Beware of the Fallacy of Nationalism
3. Mid-Autumn /Moon Festival -- the Gatherings before the Time of Coronavirus
4. A Peaceful Fighter -- Revisiting Gandhi in the Time of Coronavirus
5. The Burning Amazon
6. What's New in the New Decade
7. Get on Board, Everybody
8. Amid the Coronavirus Threat
9. Celebrating Easter Amid the Coronavirus Crisis
10. Travel with Care in the Time of Coronavirus
11. Responsible, Safe and Smart Road-Tripping
12. 1/3 of the Countries Americans Can Travel to in the Time of Coronavirus
13. United We Stand Tall and Strong
14. TikTok or Not
15. A Veteran's Day after the 2020 Election

16. An Unspeakable Day in American History
17. The Ally Policy on China
18. What to Do with Hate Crimes Against Asian Americans
19. Changing with the Times?
20. From Simplicity to Sublimity
21. Poetry in the Time of Coronavirus
22. Love in the Time of Coronavirus
23. Education in the Time of Coronavirus
24. Digital Socialization in the Time of Coronavirus
25. Things to Do in the Time of Coronavirus
26. Defying Cyberattacks in the Time of Coronavirus
27. Lessons from the Time of Coronavirus
28. Democracy in the Time of Coronavirus
29. Coming Together for Global Peace and Growth (Reprint)
30. Are We Prepared for the Next Pandemic?

Appendix:
The Benefit of Diversity (Reprint)
Discussion Questions for *The Un-death of Me* (Reprint)
Thank you for Reading!
About the Author

Writings in the Time of Coronavirus

Global Competence Revisited

1. Globalization in the Time of Coronavirus

The cultural dynamics of globalization have always implied viral, speedy effects on the world. While mostly a positive force to uphold global collaboration in finance, economy, as well as industrial, scientific, and technological development, globalization also brings about problematic and unjust expansion or colonialism. Criticism of globalization grows with outbreaks of HIV, the swine flu, mad cow disease, SARS, influenzas, and presently -- COVID-19. The Coronavirus pandemic evokes crucial questions we must ask ourselves: why and how should we ensure globalization works to our advantage?

Clearly globalization is not going away. As the anthropologist Appadurai points out: "Though many nation-states are preoccupied with tightening their borders, maximizing their medical resources and prioritizing the health of their citizens above all else, no country has taken any serious action to undo or reverse their global alliances, interests and strategies." Indeed, cooperation among nations to handle the pandemic is inevitable and key to defeating Coronavirus. The rampant contagion has prompted a need to reshape a world where both globalization and anti-globalization pressures remain enduring. Globalization and opposition to globalization will present new opportunities and challenges to pave the road to recovery and boost international flows.

How, then, in the next round of interconnecting activities, can the world envision a new light that shines brighter for the destiny of mankind? We must learn from the pandemic experiences -- we must examine the impacts of COVID-19 on globalization and readjust relevant courses: trade, travel, mobility, economy, food, supply chains, resources, jobs, education, entertainment, sports, and healthcare systems – all aspects of human life. We must take the lessons to heart.

Mr. Faiola of the Washington Post states: "The golden era of globalization brought prosperity, but it also brought hubris." In the 1990s, globalization has emerged to warrant economic and cultural growth through urbanization and interconnectedness of the world. Globalization created many opportunities and enhanced human interaction. However, it has never halted xenophobia or marginalization of vulnerable groups. Many right-wing populists are using the Coronavirus crisis to instigate racist attacks or incite further prejudices (look at the USA in the 2020 elections, as well as Brazil and India to find brazen examples).

We must learn from the pandemic experiences -- we must examine the impacts of COVID-19 on globalization and readjust relevant courses: trade, travel, mobility, economy, food, supply chains, resources, jobs, education,

entertainment, sports, and healthcare systems – all aspects of human life. We must take the lessons to heart.

As it turned out in the late 2000s, the world witnessed a grandiose bubble burst in the housing and finance markets, caused by over-spending, frantic borrowing, toxic financial instruments, and weak regulations. Dreams of prosperity, when misconstrued, drained personal savings and national reserves.

The world is eager and will open for business again. People, companies, and countries will return to do business with one another. But the way we work, consume, invest, socialize, travel, and cooperate on global issues has changed forever. As a matter of fact, the right change is very much needed, and the battle will continue beyond the time of Coronavirus.

(Originally published on https://aacs.website/wp-content/uploads/2021/06/AACSNL6.9.21.pdf)

2. Beware of the Fallacy of Nationalism

While white supremacists defend racist rhetoric or attacks out of fear and hate of being outnumbered in a diverse society, while discriminatory and even cruel policies are established evidencing protectionism outweighs humanistic principles, and while white terrorism rampages in the United States -- it is crucial to reexamine nationalism and discern its implications for the world. Nationalism could relate to the feel of patriotism and pride about one's own country, culture, ethnicity, values, or achievements. It could lead to superiority complex or to an extreme degree, justification of supremacy. Nationalism promotes development of national infrastructure and economy, provides motivations for hard work, strength and success. On the other hand, nationalism induces alienation from the global community due to isolationism and self-interest. It also evokes further separation of individuals based on finance, ethnicity, religion, or social status. In its severe form, nationalism leads to warring cliques, race groups, sub-nations, and countries.

Without careful deliberation and discussion to balance nationalist outlooks, unity in diversity will break as in modern-today America, where white nationalism grows, and intolerance increases. The extent of resistance, prejudice or bigotry could lead to hate and instigate treacherous catastrophes. Albert Einstein determined in his lifetime: "Nationalism is an infantile disease. It is the measles of mankind." He also declared: "I am against any nationalism, even in the guise of mere patriotism. Privileges based on position and property have always seemed to me unjust and pernicious, as did any exaggerated personality cult." History is full of examples to verify Einstein's remark. German leaders, such as Hitler, instituted anti-Jew laws, brainwashed citizens, and was able to rationalize one of the worst genocides in the history of mankind.

One imminent task of every responsible citizen is to detect the fallacy of nationalism, condemn dangerous nationalist movements or trends, and to avert new hate by learning from America's entrenched old hate. 600 extremists around the country attended the white supremacist "Unite the Right" rally in Charlottesville, Virginia, on August 11-12, 2017. Its deadly violent end did not "save" the white race, but incited crime and unspeakable animosity. According to ADL's report, "White supremacists have killed more people in recent years than any other type of domestic extremist (54% of all domestic extremist-related murders in the past 10 years). They are also a troubling source of domestic terror incidents (including 13 plots or attacks within the past five years)." Incidents of white terroristic mass shootings, for example in El Passo, TX in August 2019, are signaling alarming social trends. If this is not the time to review the lessons of history, when would it be?

White nationalism may be different from "white supremacy," but the unrealistic desire to live among and with only their own race, in a so-called white "ethnostate," can be just as misleading and fallacious. While one acknowledges this type of ideology, one needs to recognize that ethnic dominance must not lead to vicious exclusion of others. As a matter of fact, racially homogenous societies simply do not exist and need not die or kill for. The enterprise of our time should be one that seeks to dissolve and resolve conflicts and disagreements derived from diversity, or any such disparity existing in any community, be it homogeneous or heterogeneous. Boundaries of races or nations need not and could not be built only to deny its essence and existence; they are better to be bridged with gumption, integrity, and soul.

Boundaries of races or nations need not and could not be built only to deny its essence and existence; they are better to be bridged with gumption, integrity, and soul.

(Originally published on https://aacs.website/wp-content/uploads/2019/08/AACSNL8.5.19.pdf)

3. **Mid-Autumn /Moon Festival -- the Gatherings before the Time of Coronavirus**

The 15th day of the eighth lunar month, the closest full moon day to the Autumnal Equinox, marks the Mid-Autumn Festival, or Moon Festival. It is one of the most important fetes in East and Southeast Asia. During the festival, families reunite to watch the fullest moon of the year, eating mooncakes, lighting lanterns, and celebrating harvests.

The Moon Festival originated from ancient Chinese's offerings to the moon and hosting a great feast. Legend has it that the fearless Chinese archer Hou Yi shot down nine surplus suns to protect the world. He was rewarded with an elixir from heaven.

Hou Yi's wife Chang'e drank the elixir and floated to the moon.

It is said that family members, near and far, are united with the same awe and admiration for the only fullest moon of the year.

On the day of the fullest moon every year, Hou Yi hoped to get a glimpse of his wife's shadow. People nowadays, gather to watch the moon, looking for Chang'e, along with Yutu (Jade Rabbit, China's moon rover -- was the legendary rabbit sent to accompany Chang'e). Moon Cake, sliced up and shared among family and friends, is used to commemorate the occasion. It is said that family members, near and far, are united with the same awe and admiration for the only fullest moon of the year.

Only that there is something particularly special about the 2019 Moon Festival. Little does the world know that family gatherings and celebrations can present a danger or threat to people's lives because social-distancing mitigation measures are required during the time of pandemics. The time of Coronavirus, which comes only a couple of months after the festivity of 2019 Moon Festival, imposes a complete lockdown and forces all congregations or get-togethers to stop.

We only realize how precious festivals and holidays are when we face the unprecedented crisis in our lifetime. If only family members, near and far, remember not to take reunions for granted. If only friends and associates, near and far, take heed of the conditions that must exist to join others in the same room, in the same car, on the same train, or in any proximity of one another. We need to hold the time of togetherness dear and appreciate how lovely it is to be able to "get together." When we come back and gather, we shall be forever grateful!

(Originally published on https://aacs.website/wp-content/uploads/2019/09/AACSNL9.14.19.pdf)

4. A Peaceful Fighter -- Revisit Gandhi in the Time of Coronavirus

Born on October 2nd, 1869, Mahatma Gandhi was India's icon for non-violent battle to attain independence from Britain, as well as unity of India. A peaceful fighter he was -- the oxymoron within inevitably foretold unsettled sectarian tension between Muslims and Hindu people. Such struggles continue to this day. In October of 2019 as many world leaders paid tribute to Gandhi's 150th birthday, his portrait was reportedly defaced. The assailants of Gandhi's legacy were subsequently under investigation.

The case alleged "imputations, assertions prejudicial to national integration," "intentional insult with an intent to provoke the breach of peace," and "statements conducing public mischief." It revealed that not everyone in India loves Gandhi for promoting Hindu-Muslim unity. Hindu extremist, Nathuram Godse, in January 1948, assassinated the non-violent leader soon after India gained independence from British colonial rule in August 1947. The fight about ideological or religious differences remains for as long as mankind exists, and oftentimes it is not very peaceful.

In the time of Coronavirus, it is particularly important to revisit Gandhi's teachings, not only for the sake of our young generations, but for the blind or closed-minded that divert from progress or civilization. Life lessons about peace, non-violence, honesty, and integrity formulate the groundwork of reconstructing a healthy society. *"Be the change you wish to see in the world"* -- as Gandhi has taught us. When reflecting on our own weakness and strength, we can grow to be well-rounded citizens. When we change ourselves to be better versions of people for the world, perhaps the world can then become a better place for all.

In the time of Coronavirus, it is particularly important to revisit Gandhi's teachings, not only for the sake of our young generations, but for the blind or closed-minded that divert from progress or civilization.

It is unbelievable how many mass shootings and riots in the soil of America we have witnessed during the most trying time while we deal with Covid-19. The vicious cycle of violence does not solve any problems in society. We need to be better as a people. Remember the foundation of building a healthy society; we have a yet a long way to go.

(Originally published on https://aacs.website/wp-content/uploads/2019/10/AACSNL10.10.19.pdf)

5. DACA and America's Immigration Policy Reform

On June 15, 2012, President Obama announced the policy of Deferred Action for Childhood Arrivals (DACA) to enable individuals brought to the US as children to obtain a renewable two-year period of deferred action from deportation and become eligible for a work permit (but no path to citizenship). The DREAM Act (Development, Relief, and Education for Alien Minors Act), proposed for a process to grant residency and subsequently naturalized status to qualifying immigrants who entered the United States as minors. The bill was first introduced in the Senate on August 1, 2001; it has since been filibustered several times and failed to pass. In 2017, President Trump announced a plan to phase out DACA, but such implementation was put on hold for six months to allow Congress time to pass the Dream Act or some other legislative protection for Dreamers. Congress failed to act, and the time extension expired on March 5, 2018. The phase-out of DACA has been put on hold by several courts.

Trump's case to terminate DACA was brought to the Supreme Court on Tuesday November 12, 2019. After years of uncertainty and political stalemates, this was a crucial moment for Dreamers and the DACA program that protected them. If justices supported the administration's decision to end the program, those who were shielded by DACA for years could lose their work permits and become vulnerable to deportation. The implication of such decision not only involved Dreamers' fate -- it would indicate that it would be deemed unlawful for future administrations to implement such policies to filter or prioritize which groups of unlawful immigrants to deport or to allow for path to naturalization.

Research shows that DACA increased the wages and employment status of DACA-eligible immigrants, and improved lives for DACA participants and their children. Research also suggests it reduced the number of undocumented immigrant households living in poverty. "This is inarguably the most successful immigration policy," claims Harvard professor Roberto Gonzales. His study finds that DACA has provided many long-term benefits to the more than 700,000 young immigrant adults, consequently fueling the nation's workforce, and contributing to the economy. Many will agree with Professor Gonzales and recognizes DACA as consequential, and economically beneficial. David J. Skorton, a cardiologist and president and CEO of the Association of American Medical Colleges, states that ending DACA will harm America's health, since the country relies on DACA immigrants for a pool of medical or health professionals. Apple's CEO Tim Cook says in a brief that his company employs hundreds of recipients of DACA and that DREAMERS "embody Apple's innovation strategy." Cook defends DACA wholeheartedly.

While "DACA has been overwhelmingly successful, it is a partial solution," suggests Professor Gonzales. "Ultimately, DACA is an administrative policy that in nature is temporary." To preserve the protections in place for contributing immigrants, it is imperative to pass much needed policies that extend paths to naturalization. After all, the Trump administration and many DACA supporters agree that Congress could pass a comprehensive immigration reform bill that includes Dreamer protections, and their rectified channels of lawfulness.

To preserve the protections in place for contributing immigrants, it is imperative to pass much needed policies that extend paths to naturalization.

Note: A Supreme Court decision on the matter was reached in 2020: "On June 18, 2020, the U.S. Supreme Court issued a 5-4 decision finding that the Trump administration's termination of Deferred Action for Childhood Arrivals (DACA) was (1) judicially reviewable and (2) done in an arbitrary and capricious manner, in violation of the Administrative Procedure Act (APA)."

(Originally published on https://aacs.website/wp-content/uploads/2019/11/AACSNL11.11.19.pdf)

6. The Burning Amazon

For more than 10 years, men have been burning the Amazon rainforest for cattle ranching. While deforestation is also connected to commercial activities for lumber, soy, paper and palm, the cattle industry is responsible for up to 80 percent of the clearings. Call it progress or greed and lawlessness -- however you view the burning of the Amazon, the immense scale of the fires, especially in Brazil, post serious ecological threats.

In 2009, the three biggest Brazilian meatpacking companies, JBS, Minerva and Marfrig, signed an agreement with the environmental group Greenpeace not to buy cattle from ranchers from newly deforested areas. But the vows have been only partially kept and manipulated via the complicated supply chain.

An estimated 173,746 square miles of forest -- the size of California, plus Massachusetts and New Jersey -- have been converted to cattle pasture, according to the Yale School of Forestry. Ranch farming has generated over $6 billion in annual export revenues and about 360,000 jobs in Brazil. As livestock might be bought and sold multiple times until it reached the ranch that sold it directly to a slaughterhouse, most of the Amazon ranches that sold cattle directly to JBS, Marfrig and Minerva were essentially middlemen. Those middlemen aggregated cattle from various inadequately regulated farms, according to data from University of Wisconsin. The supply chain has made the phenomenon of "cattle laundering" common and created a roadblock to fulfilling the Greenpeace agreement. Greenpeace pulled out of the agreement in 2017.

After Greenpeace, Brazilian federal prosecutors signed a deal with 13 additional national meatpackers allowing federal law enforcement officers to monitor the source of their cattle, so that slaughterhouses would relinquish ties with deforesting cattlemen. Eventually, about 100 signed on, including the Big 3.

The deal did lead to improvements, as the meatpacking companies established the protocols to monitor their suppliers. On the other hand, limited amount of new land for grazing has increased demand for beef, both domestically and internationally. The result was a surge in the cattle laundering practice that has undermined the deals.

At present, none of the meat packing companies are making substantial efforts to track their suppliers. With the far-right politicians in power, boosting the economy takes precedence other environmental agenda. In the future, we are likely to witness more forest fire and further deforestation. The Amazon is continually on fire and would not cease burning in the foreseeable future.

In the future, we are likely to witness more forest fire and further deforestation. The Amazon is continually on fire and would not cease burning in the foreseeable future.

(Originally published on https://aacs.website/wp-content/uploads/2019/12/AACSNL12.17.19.pdf)

7. What's New in the New Decade

Will this be the decade where we finally take control of our destiny or will this be another decade of the "same old same old" -- where the rich get richer, and the planet continues to fall into a state of disrepair? Will the lessons of Covid-19 make any differences?

The year of 2020 kicked off the beginning of a new decade. What's new? -- you asked at the dawn of the new era. Little did one know the time of Coronavirus was upon the world and everything would never be the same as before. While no one can make 100% accurate predictions of what's in store for mankind, you could discern what's planned in the new decade. Japan would hold the Summer Olympics (or not) while also endeavoring to build a robotic moon base. Many countries would have major elections, including America where Trump's legacy would be determined. The tallest building in the world would be Jeddah Tower in Saudi Arabia, upon its completion. Chips would be implanted in human brains, cars would drive themselves, and -- China would venture to build the longest high-speed rail from Beijing to London (yes, China is still expanding its power during the peak of Coronavirus spread in 2021. A rocket was launched without the country knowing where it would land: "The Chinese rocket has come down. The 23-ton core stage of a Long March 5B booster crashed back to Earth Saturday night (May 8), ending 10 controversial days aloft that captured the attention of the world and started a wider conversation about orbital debris and responsible spacefaring.").

Among so many new happenings in technology, economy, politics, and the Covid-19 pandemic, the determining factor of human destiny, for the most part, relies upon
America's election of a new president. The new president would have a profound impact on America's role on the world stage: reclaiming trust or deepening the disasters we witness around the world. So it happened, President Biden has turned the world around within the first couple months of his presidency in 2021!

In any case, would the world find peace? Would the hungry get fed? Would the homeless be taken care of? Would climate change be looked at seriously by the world leaders? All these questions may be at the forefront of what the populace is looking for in this new decade. Certainly, those issues were leading the mainstream media in popularity at the beginning of the new decade. And then, Covid-19 brought the world to its knees!

As the world brace for unprecedented technological explorations – and the pandemic, perhaps wonders of the past decades could steer us clear of wrong or harmful choices. On a personal level, let's revere the resolutions of bettering ourselves. From a global standpoint, may our lens be open wide enough to look at the whole planet, its health, and the greater wellbeing of the world's populations. We need to remove/eliminate tyrannical regimes, remove power-mongering world leaders, sideline the need for greater personal wealth by the already incredibly rich, and focus on the real issues, the real long-term problems we must overcome, in order to have a healthy planet and population.

Will this be the decade where we finally take control of our destiny or will this be another decade of the "same old same old" -- where the rich get richer, and the planet continues to fall into a state of disrepair? Will the lessons of Covid-19 make any differences?

(Originally published on https://aacs.website/wp-content/uploads/2020/01/AACSNL1.5.20.pdf)

7. Get on Board, Everybody

Sanna Mirella Marin has been serving as Finland's Prime Minister since December 10, 2019. A Social Democrat at age 34, she is not only the world's youngest serving state leader but Finland's youngest prime minister. Her all-women governing cabinet of 5 parities speaks for how far Finland's social equality has developed. The United States, as a world leader of developed countries, pales in comparison as far as its citizens' engagement with dimensions of social justice, be it gender or racial equality. Finland was the first country in the world to elect women to parliament over a century ago. Many other countries in the world also have had female leaders, such as England, India, Austria, Taiwan, Brazil, Ukraine, to name a few. Women or any other candidates of various backgrounds should not be judged based on their gender, sexual orientation, age, race, or economic status. A leader is to lead with character, vision, and coalition from all sides.

I

A leader is o lead with character, vision, and coalition from all sides.

Commentators have cast Marin as the antidote to strongman world leaders. As the world watches how Marin tackles, everybody should get on board in the United States amidst its own country's political debates and partisan divides, to rethink what opportunities or choices the American people are allowing themselves to have in future elections.

Do we judge and choose wisely, or do we let our bias or greed steer our destiny? Do we need a divider or a principled leader? Do we side with dictatorship, or do we stand up for our own freedom? Do we vote solely for illusive money pockets, or do we vote for a meaningful, healthy, and prosperous life? Do we want a pompous showman, or do we hope for a solid, genuine humanitarian to rebuild, and to restore our sense of justice?

Many Americans appear to be still very much at war with their own conscience -- even after the 2020 election. We have our work cut out for us to strive for an America that is the quintessential "land of the free and home of the brave."

(Originally published on https://aacs.website/wp-content/uploads/2020/02/AACSNL2.9.20.pdf

8. Amid the Coronavirus Threat

Amid the Coronavirus/Covid-19 threat, the world is taking measures to avoid public gatherings or mass events. The Coachella Valley Music and Arts Festival is postponed to October in 2020, Austin cancels South by Southwest Festival, NBA and NHL both halt their sport seasons, conventions throughout are either cancelled or rescheduled, and the House also prepares for telework scenarios. People around the globe are at risk and bracing for the worst. Should you then, take that trip you planned months ago? The answer depends on where you're going and how cautious and knowledgeable you are about the contagion.

As experts point out, testing and isolation, not travel bans, are what we need against Coronavirus. Do take precautions when traveling, though. Equip yourself with updated, accurate information and stay clear of potential contagious sources.

No matter where you are or where you travel to, the most important thing is to stay healthy and clean: eating right, sleeping plenty, washing your hands with regular soap or using an alcohol-based hand sanitizer after being exposed to/touching any public surface.

There are four travel advisory levels: Level 4 -- do not travel; Level 3 -- reconsider travel; Level 2 -

- exercise increased caution; and Level 1 -- exercise normal precautions. The countries listed below require particular caution if/when you're travelling.

As of March 12, 2020, countries that are now under the category of Level 4: Do Not Travel, include China and Iran, according to the Department of State's travel advisory. Other non-coronavirus risk indicators, including terrorism, kidnapping, and armed conflict involve: Haiti, Iraq, Mali, Central African Republic, Venezuela, Yemen, South Sudan, Burkina Faso, Syria, Somalia, Afghanistan, North Korea, and Libya.

Italy, South Korea, and Mongolia are at Level 3 -- Reconsider Travel. Italy and Iran are among the countries with the largest numbers of cases outside Asia. Other non-coronavirus risk indicators, including terrorism, kidnapping, and armed conflict involve: Pakistan, Burundi, Democratic Republic of the Congo, Niger, Nigeria, Lebanon, Guinea-Bissau, Chad, Sudan, Honduras, and Nicaragua.

Japan, Hong Kong, Macau are listed at Level 2: Exercise Increased Caution. Other non-coronavirus risk indicators, including crimes, civil unrest, and arbitrary enforcement of local laws involve: Ukraine, Guinea, Russia, Serbia, Timore-Leste, Brazil, Costa Rica, Bolivia, Nepal, Azerbaijan, Indonesia, Mauritania, South Africa, Belgium, Mexico, Sierra Leone, Tanzania, The Bahamas, Tajikistan, Dominica, Cuba, Chile, Ecuador, Peru, Spain, Papua New Guinea, Myanmar (Burma), El Salvador, Saudi Arabia, Turkey, Malawi, Ethiopia, Cote d'lvoire, Uruguay, Netherlands, Madagascar, Egypt, Denmark, Bosnia and Herzegovina, Sri Lanka, Germany, Kosovo, Guyana, Zimbabwe, Maldives, United Kingdom, Republic of the Congo, Jamaica, Dominican Republic, Uganda, Trinidad and Tobago, Philippines, Kenya, Colombia, Cameroon, Bangladesh, Algeria, Morocco, France, India, Guatemala, Turks and Caicos Islands, Eritrea, Antarctica, Belize, Tunisia, Israel, and Jordan.

Countries listed at Level 1: Exercise Normal Precautions are: Thailand, Palau, Solomon Island, Micronesia, Luxembourg, Australia, Slovenia, Montenegro, Poland, Croatia, Canada, The Kyrgyz Republic, Samoa, Armenia, Zambia, Namibia, Lesotho, Eswatini, Botswana, North Macedonia, Seychelles, Mauritius, Fiji, The Gambia, Rwanda, Equatorial Guinea, Cabo Verde, Bulgaria, Austria, New Zealand, French Guiana, Djibouti, Tonga, Kiribati, Ireland, Brunei, Belarus, Suriname, Switzerland, Liechtenstein, Laos, Finland, Norway, Andorra, Hungary, Cyprus, Romania, Estonia, Slovakia, Latvia, Moldova, Ghana, Albania, Greece, Malta, Czech Republic, Iceland, Lithuania, Portugal, Benin, Togo, United Arab Emirates, Qatar, Oman, Kuwait, Bahrain, Saint Kitts and Nevis, British Virgin Islands, Anguilla, Panama, Comoros, Turkmenistan, Saint Lucia, Malaysia, Georgia, Angola, Kazakhstan, Nauru, New Caledonia, Sweden, French Polynesia, Vanuatu, Barbados, Saint Vincent and The Grenadines, Montserrat, Antigua and Barbuda, Tuvalu, Grenada, French West Indies, Mozambique,

Bhutan, Paraguay, Sao Tome and Principle, Gabon, Sint Maarten, Curacao, Cayman Islands, Bonaire, Sint Eustatius, Saba, Bermuda, Aruba, Liberia, Cambodia, Vietnam, Taiwan, Singapore, Uzbekistan, Marshall Islands, and Argentina.

Coronavirus spreads through respiratory droplets through proximity, contact, and the surfaces upon which the droplets land -- like airplane seats and tray tables. The University of Chicago Medicine defines exposure as being within six feet of an infected person for 10 minutes or longer. How long those droplets last depends both on the droplet and the surface -- mucus or saliva, porous or non-porous. To a lesser degree, respiratory viruses can also be transmitted through the air in tiny, dry particles known as aerosols. Viruses like moisture, and many fade from being infectious if left dry for too long.

No matter where you are or where you travel to, the most important thing is to stay healthy and clean: eating right, sleeping plenty, washing your hands with regular soap or using an alcohol-based hand sanitizer after being exposed to/touching any public surface. While on a plane, sit at the window seats to avoid exposure to the virus or close contact with others. Limit your own movement throughout the airplane; do not touch your face, eyes, mouth, or nose with unwashed hands. Follow the public health measures and hope for the best.

(Originally published on https://aacs.website/wp-content/uploads/2020/03/AACSNL3.20.20.pdf)

9. Celebrating Easter Amid the Coronavirus Crisis

Easter 2020 (April 12) accentuates how people are adjusting to the new order of staying home and manifesting human resilience in ingenious celebrations.

Easter, or Resurrection Sunday, commemorates the resurrection of Jesus from the dead. Easter and holidays related to it -- such as Ash Wednesday, Palm Sunday, and Good Friday -- are called "movable feasts." They do not fall on fixed dates on the Gregorian calendar but follow a lunisolar calendar. The date of Easter is set for the first Sunday following the first full Moon of spring, which occurs on or shortly after the Spring Equinox.

Celebrated around the world, Easter is one of the most important holidays. But in 2020, Easter celebrations look very different as more than 1.5 billion people worldwide have been asked to stay home amid the Coronavirus crisis. However constrained the world is, the spring finds its way to shine all the same. People are maintaining some semblance of normalcy and sharing this holiday in creative ways.

Easter 2020 (April 12) accentuates how people are adjusting to the new order of staying home and manifesting human resilience in ingenious celebrations. Eggs, bunnies, treats, spring-like decorations are either bought online or created at home. People are meeting virtually or at a safe distance, collaborating via live streaming events: window displays of decorated eggs or arts, singing together but apart on videos, for example.

While people forego large public Easter egg hunts and face-to-face gatherings with family, they uphold the Easter spirit together, though physically apart. Let's remember that the virus can be transmitted by people who are not showing symptoms, according to the US Centers for Disease Control and Prevention. Let's fight the desire to socialize during these tying times. With imagination, with love, and luckily with the help of technology, we are in this together, and for sure, will come out of it stronger than ever.

(Originally published on https://aacs.website/wp-content/uploads/2020/04/AACSNL4.8.20.pdf)

10. Travel with Care in the Time of Coronavirus

Covid-19 has undoubtedly devastated the travel industry and changed the ways we would travel in the foreseeable future. 100 million travel sector jobs has been lost, according to one global estimate. Use of U.S. airlines is down 95 percent, while international travel revenues would decrease by more than $300 billion. Safety issues concerning travels are at the forefront as the desire to travel remains. The most pressing questions about future travels concern coordination of social distancing measures, testing and healthcare strategies, space and distance creations, as well as innovative procedures for travelers and industry providers alike.

Many travel providers have implemented necessary redesigns to ensure or improve safe travels. Testing, health screening, control of space-per-passenger ratios, and a redesign of passenger flow or even airport layouts are some of the changes we will witness when we eventual get to travel. Expansive new airports will offer passengers more space; airports without the capacity to expand horizontally may expand vertically. Furthermore, gate space will be widened, and robots may be used to load carry-ons. Disinfection protocols will be in place, and travel industry personnel or travelers will be expected to don personal protective equipment or masks.

Road tripping offers a sense of freedom with personal controls and are on the rise.

Travel avenues and destinations are likely to transform. Road tripping offers a sense of freedom with personal controls and are on the rise. Travel industry suppliers offer more flexibility, more discounts, and better rates; listings for accommodations will indicate whether operators/ hosts are practicing stringent cleaning/distancing guidelines, including a minimum 24-hour waiting period between bookings. Hygiene and cleanliness will become the new rating criteria whereas typically food or the view from a hotel room drives the sales. More touchless check-in via apps and drive-up motel rooms will gain popularity. Many national parks and remote outdoor areas are attracting record numbers. People touring these destinations will seek personal space, cleanliness, and fresh air.

As international travel is considered riskier and unpredictable, it will become even more time-consuming and expensive. As a result, domestic tourism as well as private/remote tours will experience a boost. New opportunities lie in times of crises, and so plan and adjust according to changes.

Prepare carefully and wisely for a time when things reopen and recover.

(Originally published on https://aacs.website/wp-content/uploads/2020/05/AACSNL5.11.20.pdf)

11. Responsible, Safe and Smart Road-Tripping

With COVID-19 airborne and threatening to infect more people, Americans are leery of indoor/air travel. Instead, road-tripping is back -- the adventurous spirit of Kerouac and Steinbeck returns, and the great outdoors awaits. Americans are blessed with a car culture that expresses a sense of freedom, but that blessing is now mixed with challenges and roadblocks during this time of a global pandemic.

There are certain worries as you take your road trips: the increase of the chance of being infected or unknowingly spreading the virus; how hotels or places of accommodation take precautionary procedures; how people you come across behave during the pandemic. You may also be stopped at the state borders and have unusual inquiries from officials: where you are going; where you traveled from; who is traveling with you, etc. (According to July 2020 regulations, Maine and New

Mexico requires some out-of-state and international travelers to quarantine for two weeks upon arrival. Florida requires travelers to complete informational surveys detailing their vacation plans.) However, the quandary of road-tripping will subside as you educate yourself about the roads as well as the virus.

With careful planning/reservations and precautionary observations of your surroundings, you can happily road-trip like before. Know the routes you take involve what kind of case numbers and relevant state regulations; take the road less traveled; always wear a mask in public; wash and sanitize your hands; social distance. You may have a few extra items to pack, such as sanitizers, disinfectant wipes, cleaning products, emergency kits, as well as food items to avoid eating out too much. Exercise caution when you absolutely need to use a public restroom; wait before you use a stall someone just used. You can never be too careful.

There are many websites and apps that provide useful information regarding best routes, campsites, drive-throughs, restaurants, take-outs, curbside pickups, gas costs, or any travel needs you may have. Google Maps or GPS may be good enough if you have a small vehicle and want to stay on the main roads; research scenic routes or byways if you're in the mood for roadside adventures. Research best routes for comfort and safety if you drive a RV (RV LIFE app provides turn-by-turn directions safely around unforeseen obstacles like low-hanging bridges or narrow highways). The key is to plan before you hit the road, knowing that your cellphone may be offline on the road. With enough planning and a little spontaneity, you can be a responsible, safe, and smart road-tripper. Happy Trails.

The quandary of road-tripping will subside as you educate yourself about the roads as well as the virus.

(Originally published on https://aacs.website/wp-content/uploads/2020/07/AACSNL7.6.20.pdf)

12. 1/3 of the Countries Americans Can Travel to in the Time of Coronavirus

With 6.5 million Covid-19 cases and 194K deaths, many countries barred U.S. travelers -- understandably. While most nations in E.U and Asia closed their doors on Americans, there were about 1/3 of the World's countries where Americans could travel to as of September 2020 (America's Covid death rate was the world's highest at the end of 2020 at approximately 14%, with more than 20 million case. In 2021, Biden's successful rollout of vaccines has saved the country. Upon the time of this book's publication in the summer of 2021, there are about 34,340,000 cases and 615,300 deaths in the US, with a death rate of 1.8%):

1. Albania – July 1
2. Anguilla – August 21
3. Antigua and Barbuda – June 4

4. Armenia – August 12
5. Aruba – July 10
6. Bahamas – July 1(with Negative Covid-19 Test Proof)
7. Barbados – July 12
8. Bali (Indonesia) September 1
9. Belarus – July 15
10. Belize – August 15
11. Bermuda – July 1
12. Brazil – July 30
13. Bulgaria – Restrictions (with Negative Covid-19 Test Proof)
14. Cambodia – July 15 ($2000 USD Deposit Required for Testing and Relevant Costs)
15. Canada - Restrictions (with A Mandatory Quarantine or Self-isolation Period)
16. Cayman Islands – September 1
17. Costa Rica – September 1
18. Croatia – July 1 (with Negative Covid-19 Test Proof)
19. Dominica – August 7
20. Dominican Republic – July 1
21. Dubai (UAE) – July 7
22. Ecuador – August 16

23. Egypt – August 15 (with Negative Covid-19 Test Proof)
24. Ethiopia – (with A Mandatory Quarantine or Self-isolation Period)
25. French Polynesia – July 15
26. Ghana – September 1
27. Grenada – August 1
28. Haiti – July 1
29. Honduras – August 17
30. Ireland – (with A Mandatory Quarantine or Self-isolation Period)
31. Jamaica – June 15
32. Kenya – August (with Negative Covid-19 Test Proof)
33. Maldives – July 15
34. Malta – July 11 (pending exception approval)
35. Mexico – June 8; September 21to Open Land Borders
36. Montenegro – August 15
37. Morocco – September 6 (with Negative Covid-19 Test Proof)
38. Nicaragua – October 1
39. North Macedonia – July 1

40. Romania – Restrictions (with Negative Covid-19 Test Proof)
41. Rwanda – June 17; August 1 for Americans (with Negative Covid-19 Test Proof)
42. Serbia – May 22 (with Negative Covid-19 Test Proof)
43. St. Bart's – June 22
44. St. Barthélemy – (with A Mandatory Quarantine or Self-isolation Period)
45. St. Lucia – June 4 (with Negative Covid-19 Test Proof)
46. St. Maarten – August 1 (with Negative Covid-19 Test Proof)
47. St. Vincent and The Grenadines – July 1
48. South Korea – (with A Mandatory Quarantine or Self-isolation Period)
49. Tanzania – June 1
50. Turkey – June 12
51. Turks and Caicos – July 22 (with Negative Covid-19 Test Proof)
52. Ukraine – July 20
53. United Arab Emirates – July 7 (with Negative Covid-19 Test Proof)

54. United Kingdom – (with A Mandatory Quarantine or Self-isolation Period)
55. Zambia – July
56. Zimbabwe – October 1 (with Negative Covid-19 Test Proof)

American passports were not very popular at one point in time! It is interesting to witness how one's life does connect to the country's status or destiny. Other than the usual research one conducts for travels, extra precautions must be taken to observe the country-specific levels of travel advice (with levels from 1-4 depending on country-specific conditions). Country-specific regulations and restrictions also requires extra examination and planning. Stay safe and strong!

American passports were not very popular at one point in time! It is interesting to witness how one's life does connect to the country's status or destiny.

(Originally published on https://aacs.website/wp-content/uploads/2020/09/AACSNL9.13.20.pdf)

13. United We Stand Tall and Strong

During these times of civil unrest, we need to think hard and clear about what it means to be American. Peaceful measures, instead of looting and destruction, should formulate our channels of expression.

As if the COVID-19 pandemic were not devastating already, 2020 America should have to experience yet another upheaval. Protests about police brutality and inequality/injustice have broken out in all corners across the United States, from Minneapolis, New York, Philadelphia, Washington D.C., Atlanta, Miami, to Louisville, Houston, Cincinnati, Las Vegas, Los Angeles, Sacramento, and Seattle, etc. Following George Floyd's tragic decease under a chokehold by a police officer that went seriously wrong, the unrelenting issues of racism resurface and drive large crowds to gather and demonstrate despite the need for social distancing and economic recovery.

The world seems to have come to its horrific end, or at least the world as we know it: "Not only is the nation facing current crises of public health, the economy, race relations and public safety, and perhaps democracy itself, but there are still things that could happen, … such as a foreign conflict or cyber-attack." (And so cyberattacks actually increased! See "Cyberattacks in the Time of Coronavirus.") While protests turn violent and chaotic, police have shot rubber bullets and tear-gassed both protesters and journalists, and on the other hand, unruly civilians have disrespected law enforcers, some assaulting the police. But we do not need to have more bloodshed and carnage. What we need is unity. We need to unite to solve problems and rebuild our country as well as the world. Unity is strength.

During these times of civil unrest, we need to think hard and clear about what it means to be American. Peaceful measures, instead of looting and destruction, should formulate our channels of expression. In several cities, individual police officers have knelt with protesters to covey pain over system injustices. Some have marched with protesters, while among demonstrators and the police force, there have been plenty of greetings and handshakes. Former President Obama "condemns violence, outlines how protesters can bring about real change." In his essay dated June 1, 2020, he urges our countrymen to "channel our justifiable anger into peaceful, sustained, and effective action, …and [elicit] a real turning point in our nation's long journey to live up to our highest ideals." Joe Biden also pinpoints: "George Floyd's last words [I can't breathe] … didn't die with him…. It's a wake-up call for our nation. For all of us." Our founding fathers taught us the principles of liberty/justice, and never were they parallel to violence or hostility.

"This is the United States of America. And there is nothing we can't do. If we do it together." – Joe Biden

"We are only as strong as we are united, as weak as we are divided."
-- J.K. Rowling, Harry Potter and the Goblet of Fire

"Like a sculptor, if necessary,
carve a friend out of stone.
Realize that your inner sight is blind
and try to see a treasure in everyone."
-- Jalaluddin Rumi

United we will stand tall and strong; divided we will fall even further and harder. Celebrate similarities and embrace diversity. What makes the world rich and beautiful is the unity in diversity.

(Originally published on https://aacs.website/wp-content/uploads/2020/06/AACSNL6.3.20.pdf)

14. TikTok or Not

TikTok has been accused of collecting data on Americans and sending it to the Chinese government. China, contrarily, denounces the U.S. as intending to block Chinese technology in order to protect American companies. As former President Trump demanded a cut and Microsoft sought to purchase the popular Chinese TikTok app in August 2020, China threatened to retaliate. Tension between the two countries arose; many questions concerning cybersecurity and internet use/standards remained unanswered.

Trump demanded that the U.S. obtained a "substantial portion" of the purchase price of the TikTok's US unit from a sale of TikTok to an American company. He claimed that he woud ban the app, which is owned by China's ByteDance, if there was no sale by September 15, 2020: "The United States should get a very large percentage of that price, because we're making it possible."

(TikTok's has 80 million active American users.) Trump's request for payment to the US Treasury complicated the deal as legal experts viewed his proposal as unorthodox and in need of regulatory approval. Some say this cut was just a payback for the US and its companies, claiming China had stolen intellectual property from them. The situation grew complicated as economy, politics, foreign policies, principles of democracy, and national security all became mixed in the picture.

In addition to TikTok's US business, Microsoft was also negotiating to buy its operations in Canada, Australia, and New Zealand. In the event that the deal did not happen, Trump's ban on TikTok might start by having Apple and Google remove TikTok from their online platforms, in other words, by adding TikTok's owner ByteDance to a Commerce Department entity list, and banning US entities from working with it. An alternative was to require U.S. internet service providers to block access to TikTok's servers. Either bought or banned, TikTok was encountering a serious crash with the U.S.

TikTok's core algorithm selects videos for the central feed users upon opening the app, called the "for you page" or FYP, developed by ByteDance's Chinese engineers using a suite of shared software tools, "zhongtai," or "central platform."

Subsequently on November 12, 2020 when the TikTok ban was supposed to take effect, the court halted the intended restrictions because of an ongoing lawsuit from TikTok creators. TikTok preserved its most valuable assets, an effective algorithm and a pool of creators. Those assets are certainly not easy to acquire or transport. TikTok's core algorithm selects videos for the central feed users upon opening the app, called the "for you page" or FYP, developed by ByteDance's Chinese engineers using a suite of shared software tools, "zhongtai," or "central platform." This golden goose is what makes TikTok so addictive and compelling.

An open and global internet where data moves freely has been the belief of democracies, as opposed to China's censorship. The Trump Administration was following China's autocratic measures and assuming that the only safe computer networks and data flows reside within its own borders. That might induce a fallacy in which U.S. tech industry can simply cease to do business all over the world. That might also reveal problematic cybersecurity tactics.
To protect Americans' data, the federal government is to define more rigorous standards to address data protection protocols and consequences of breaking relevant rules.

The TikTok sale did not happen by September 15, 2020. The lesson is clear: America's cybersecurity law should steer away from that of autocratic China's. Storing data within a nation's border does not necessarily provide solutions for data breaches or security issues (See "Cyberattacks in the Time of Coronavirus). All the hullabaloos in the Trump era amounted to mere gesticulations of politicians' power play and a nations' inflated protectionism.

(Originally published on https://aacs.website/wp-content/uploads/2020/08/AACSNL8.14.20.pdf)

15. A Veteran's Day after the 2020 Election

Veteran's Day falls on a Wednesday in 2020 following the call of Biden as the President-Elect on the previous weekend. On November 11, 2020, the federal holiday is to celebrate US's military heroes, the country appears unnervingly solemn and quiet. The US government seems to be in a vacant state of power, as Trump has not made any comments about the surging cases of COVID-19 in the country, his administration has not acknowledged Biden's victory, and no ascertainment or transition has taken place, yet.

In contrast to Trump's silence (except for a flurry of lawsuits complaining about the result of the presidential election), Biden has been busy setting up task forces to address various issues such as the pandemic, the economy, healthcare, as well as the environment. He has ignited America's hopes for normalcy and democracy. He has provided a stable force poised to comfort and heal the country.

A Veteran's Day following the election demonstrates again, the stark contrast between Trump and Biden. Trump, in his first public appearance in days, ignores Arlington National Cemetery's mask requirement during a wreath-laying ceremony. Joe Biden wears double masks when paying tribute to veterans at Philadelphia's Korean War Memorial. Neither of them makes remarks during the ceremonies. But their actions speak volumes, their narratives are indeed, clear for all to hear.

He has ignited America's hopes for normalcy and democracy. He has provided a stable force poised to comfort and heal the country.

(Originally published on https://aacs.website/wp-content/uploads/2020/11/AACSNL11.11.20.pdf)

16. An Unspeakable Day in American History

How would an educator or anyone explain the chaos and riots that transpired at the U.S. Capitol in Washington, D.C on January 6, 2021.? I felt disgusted and speechless in terms of America's complex and long history of racial divide or white supremacy upheld by certain groups of people (Trump supporters manifest such divide or prejudice via violence and utter disregard of our Constitution by taking over the building in a seditious attempt). While I was appalled and saddened in taciturnity, my students were calling the incident "Civil War II." Judging from the bloodshed, broken windows, terrorist symbols left inside the building, and the evidence of ammunition and explosive devices brought to our democracy's sacred ground, I recognize my students were not very far from a fair description of the reality.

While I was appalled and saddened in taciturnity, my students were calling the January 6 riot at the Capitol "Civil War II."

A teaching opportunity certainly exists. No matter where one's political view or belief resides, lawlessness or closed-mindedness is proven to be harmful and backwards. Teachable moments, however, become ever challenging for educators across the country, when morality and honesty is lacking at our country's top leadership level. How would you teach the young that bullying is a serious offense and could lead to expulsion when our political leaders are the biggest bullies of all, distorting and twisting civil processes to suit their own agenda? The manipulation of our democratic practices leading to the insurrection implies an opposing set of principles and values we preach to our students: simple kindness and respect, tolerance, civility, honesty, accountability, democratic ethics, and national security, among others.

If we continue to fail to deliver and show that words and actions have consequences, we will lose our young generations to an abyss of confusion and trauma even further. There was no justification for the actions of the Trump supporters who stormed the U.S. Capitol to disrupt the certification process of Biden's election to presidency. Let's look to the basic skill of processing anger and negative emotion through peaceful reflections and self-growth. Let's be the adults we should be and demonstrate how grown-ups should behave and bear responsibilities for their own words/actions. The past couple of years have been unprecedently difficult for everyone due to the Covid pandemic -- let's stop adding to the hardships. Let's try building back a safe society that future generations can inherit and live in. We may be as confused as the young now. We might not have all the answers -- we had better start seeking and stand up for our democracy.

(Originally published on https://aacs.website/wp-content/uploads/2021/01/AACSNL1.10.21.pdf)

17.The Ally Policy on China

The Biden administration's first talk with China took place on Saturday, February 6, 2021; crucial issues reveal gaps and differences that require US allies to fill in and provide checks and balances in the Indo-Pacific region. U.S. Secretary of State, Antony Blinken, and China's director of the Central Foreign Affairs, Yang Jiechi, discussed matters concerning Xinjiang Uighurs, Hong Kong, and Taiwan. Blinken indicated the U.S. would work with allies to hold China "accountable for its efforts to threaten stability in the Indo-Pacific, including across the Taiwan Strait." While the U.S. upheld human rights and democratic principles, the Chinese side maintained that "internal affairs" need no "foreign interferences." Such disparity in attitude would further strain the U.S.-China relations if not managed with diplomacy or creation of an optimal international environment.

Asian allies would be reengaged to cooperate and persuade China of the necessity or benefit of abiding by guidelines of international relations.

President Biden has in fact, strengthened his administration with Asia experts as the U.S. takes on China. He appointed Kurt Campbell as the National Security Council's Indo-Pacific affairs coordinator. Campbell served as assistant secretary of State for

East Asian and Pacific affairs under former President Barack Obama. He was widely recognized as a liaison to Asia. Together with Blinken, and national security advisor Jake Sullivan, he would help form U.S.'s ally policies. Asian allies would be reengaged to cooperate and persuade China of the necessity or benefit of abiding by guidelines of international relations.

The president spoke to Japanese Prime Minister Yoshihide Suga, Australian Prime Minister Scott Morrison and South Korean President Moon Jae-in, according to statements from the White House. Blinken also reached out to Japan, South Korea, Australia, the Philippines, and Thailand. While reinforcing U.S. security and commitments in the Indo-Pacific region, coalitions would be built and developed. Hopefully, China would curb its authoritarian ways and become a responsible member of the international society.

(Originally published on https://aacs.website/wp-content/uploads/2021/02/AACSNL2.7.21.pdf)

18. What to Do with Hate Crimes against Asian Americans

Since the Covid-19 pandemic, hate crimes against Asian Americans have been on the rise, as shown by a recent report by the Center for the Study of Hate and Extremism at California State University, San Bernardino: crimes against Asian Americans and Pacific Islanders (AAPI) jump by 145%. Across the United States, incidents of attacks on immigrants or people of Asian descent are raising concerns. For instance, an 84-year-old Thai immigrant in San Francisco dies after being pushed to the ground; a 61-year-old Filipino-American is slashed in the face with a box cutter on the New York subway; an 89-year-old Chinese woman is slapped and then set on fire in Brooklyn, New York; Robert Aaron Long fatally shoots eight people, including six Asian women, at spas in Atlanta, Georgia -- and the list goes on. Verbal harassments or racial slurs are widely reported (following the name-calling effect of "China virus" and "Kung Flu"), but few charges are brought against the aggressors with hate crimes.

As a result, protests take place in major cities across the country: Atlanta, Seattle, New York, Washington D.C., Chicago, Philadelphia, Honolulu, and Los Angeles, etc. And many community leaders are engaged in discussions about the hate crimes against Asian Americans. Don Lee, a community activist in New York, calls for more anti-Asian attacks to be identified as hate crimes: "Let's call it what it is. These are not random attacks." The debate over what legally constitutes anti-Asian hate crimes further reveals that the law is yet to account for ways in which Asian Americans encounter racism. Crime and punishment, policing and investigation and other coercive mechanisms may not be sufficient to stop some people from scapegoating Asian Americans. Antiracism or cultural competency education plays a key role in the public's ability to reflect on or become conscious of their own prejudice or bias. Educational or reformation institutions can work alongside national/local leaders and influencers to raise awareness about the pitfall of racism.

With collaborations at local, state, and federal levels, a holistic approach to fighting racism against Asian Americans may just intervene and correct some aberrant minds.

President Joe Biden signs an executive action banning the use of racist language within the federal government during his first week of presidency. He further issues guidance on how to respond to the increased number of anti-Asian incidents, and stresses the importance of stopping hate in his first national prime-time address on April 1, 2021: White House outlines "a plan of action that includes federal, state and local law enforcement training on handling hate crimes, establishing a committee within the COVID-19 Equity Task Force to address xenophobia against Asian people, and allocating $49.5 million to fund community-based services for Asian or Pacific Islander survivors of sexual and domestic violence."

Lawmakers and activists are also calling for more attention and resources to address the issue. California congresswoman Judy Chu, chair of the Asian Pacific American Caucus, and other legislators are urging for the US Department of Justice to "expand efforts to report, track and prosecute hate crimes." On May 18, 2021, the COVID–19 Hate Crimes Act was passed. With collaborations at local, state, and federal levels, a holistic approach to fighting racism against Asian Americans may just intervene and correct some aberrant minds.

(Originally published on https://aacs.website/wp-content/uploads/2021/04/AACSNL4.5.21.pdf)

19. Changing with the Times?

One of the most popular authors of children's books, Dr. Seuss/ Theodor Seuss Geisel has published about 60 books and sold over 700 million copies globally. As the world's viewpoints on race or stereotype evolve and advance, 6 of Dr. Seuss' books become problematically insensitive. As a result, the Seuss estate halts publications or sales of those books, including On Beyond Zebra!, Scrambled Eggs Super!, The Cat's Quizzer, McElligot's Pool and And to Think That I Saw It on Mulberry Street, which feature racial imagery or text. For example, in his debut book, *And to Think That I Saw It on Mulberry Street*, "a crude racial stereotype of an Asian man with slanted lines for eyes" was concluded to be "hurtful and wrong." The Seuss Enterprises' decision ironically drives up sales of Dr. Seuss's other books, and the 6 banned books are selling at record prices. Far from being "canceled" as Fox news declares, Dr. Seuss remains a cultural force, raising questions on many levels in the current political milieu.

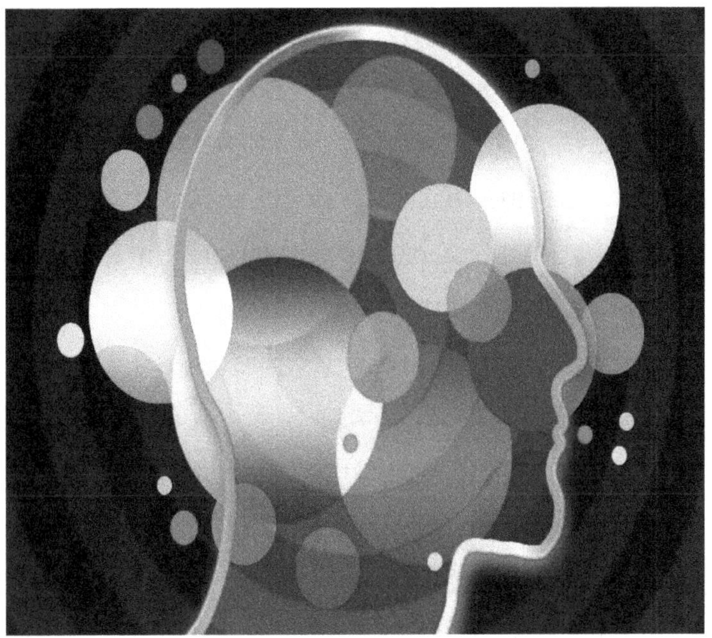

While some of Dr. Seuss' work has been criticized for its outdated or insensitive racial, ethnic, cultural and gender depictions, the author has been known to be raising awareness about cultural diversity and inclusion, humanity, and kindness, as well as care for the environment.

One of the topics of discussion on the forefront is "whether and how an author's works should be posthumously curated to reflect evolving social attitudes, and what should be preserved as part of the cultural record." While some of Dr. Seuss' work has been criticized for its outdated or insensitive racial, ethnic, cultural and gender depictions, the author has been known to be raising awareness about cultural diversity and inclusion, humanity and kindness, as well as care for the environment. Seuss passed away in 1991 and was unable to adjust his works to meet the changing marketplace. (Authors often revise their works to reflect the changing times. Roald Dahl, for instance, removed racial stereotypes in *Charlie and the Chocolate Factory*.) Dr. Seuss' estate has reviewed and updated the body of his works for him, and rightly so.

Dr. Seuss's brand is secure while cultural sensitivity is ever evolving. His masterpieces are timeless, whereas some of his works may need adjustments as times change. *Green Eggs and Ham*, *The Cat in the Hat*, and many others will endure the test of time. Readers will always be inspired by Dr.

Seuss' ethical and moral lessons; they encourage kindness and care for the people, pets, and the planet (think about themes in *Horton Hears a Who!* and *The Lorax*). No one is denouncing Dr. Seuss or "canceling" his legacy -- we can choose to use those teachable moments to show that it is perfectly O.K. for a young protagonist to show curiosity about ethnic differences, or a child to look at a pet or a unique being in a different fashion. One just needs to keep an open mind and not fall into the trap of stereotyping. It is all about learning, progressing, and using one's imagination. The question remains: do we change great works to meet the changing environment, or do we use classics to teach about how the times have changed and how at one time, things were looked at differently? Perhaps the answer to that question is as a matter of fact, beside the question. What's relevant here is mankind's collective legacy -- onward and upward!

(Originally published on https://aacs.website/wp-content/uploads/2021/03/AACSNL3.6.21.pdf)

20. From Simplicity to Sublimity

To see a World in a Grain of Sand

And a Heaven in a Wild Flower

Hold Infinity in the palm of your hand

And Eternity in an hour

. . . .

Excerpt from "Auguries of Innocence"

BY WILLIAM BLAKE

What do we have to rejoice in the time of Coronavirus? Blake's lines can be particularly inspiring at present -- in simple daily exercises that require no expertise or artistry, we shall find beauty or satisfaction and sense a purpose in a life confined and limited in so many ways. Indeed, when we behold what is around us, with a renewed sense of wonder, we shall find precious meanings and purposes.

The process of observing, creating, and self-reflecting via simple undertakings can bring us endless fulfillment and joy: a poem, a painting, an object in our surroundings, a phenomenon in nature, a dance movement, a deep breath we take, an emotion we feel, a pen we use to write, a line from some song lyrics, a beat locked in a beloved tune, a visage of someone we care, etc. We might not have a clear vision where life is going, but we will feel centered, in tune with our intuition to reidentify or uncover ourselves, and further to process our inner demons, hardships, and to engage in productivity and actions that make us whole.

When we touch, see, smell, taste, hear or feel, we form connections with others and with the world, through mental processes as well as physical engagements. We concentrate on discovering/ relearning thc ordinary and its sublimity. The best medicine derives from life's simple pleasures. Use it to heal, to sense ourselves, to act and create, and to produce -- so that we are constantly engrossed and growing.

When we behold what is around us, with a renewed sense of wonder, we shall find precious meanings and purposes.

(Originally published on https://aacs.website/wp-content/uploads/2021/05/AACSNL5.9.21.pdf)

21. Poetry in the Time of Coronavirus

Louise Glück has won the 2020 Nobel Prize in Literature "for her unmistakable poetic voice that with austere beauty makes individual existence universal," as the Swedish Academy commended. Along with Bob Dylan in 2016 and Toni Morrison in 1993, Glück was the third American to be honored with the prize in recent years. Glück, the 16th woman to win the literature prize since the Nobel prizes were first awarded in 1901, has published 12 poetry collections and several volumes of essays on poetry, with themes of childhood and family relationships, inspired by myths and classical motifs.

Previously Glück won the Pulitzer Prize in 1993 for her collection The Wild Iris, and the National Book Award in 2014. She also was awarded a 2015 National Humanities Medal by Barack Obama at the White House. Her other honors included the 2001 Bollingen Prize for Poetry, the Wallace Stevens Award, given in 2008. She was editor of the anthology The Best American Poetry 1993 and was named the United States' poet laureate in 2003.

Though Glück's dark themes -- isolation, betrayal, fractured relationships, aging, and death, present troubling aspects of human life, her refined language and allusions to mythology render her writing a universal and enduring appeal. The catharsis from reading her works transcends depressive facets of human existence. That is how her literature gives meanings to human sufferings and blunders. That is how the world, particularly during this isolated era of Covid-19, can always return to something pure and cleansed, something akin to the laureate's poetry:

At the end of my suffering
there was a door.
Hear me out: that which you call death
I remember.
("The Wild Iris")

Though Glück's dark themes -- isolation, betrayal, fractured relationships, aging, and death, present troubling aspects of human life, her refined language and allusions to mythology render her writing a universal and enduring appeal.

(Originally published on https://aacs.website/wp-content/uploads/2020/10/AACSNL10.11.20.pdf)

22. Love in the Time of Coronavirus

Online dating was popular before Coronavirus; the pandemic is making it more prevalent and inevitable. People are sifting through their matches and meeting people electronically. In person or not, romantic dates require coordination or mitigation measures between two people trying to connect. What that means is that love in the time of Coronavirus is more complicated than usual.

How can one find love in a global pandemic? Surprisingly, many have said that the pandemic helped people identify their matches with fewer distractions. The way people search for love is reinvented. People have more time to self-reflect, figure out what they really want in a mate, can get to know potential partners, and weed out candidates who do not match with them more effectively through virtual meetings. They set clear expectations and boundaries from the onset with more clarity. They may know quickly what mitigation measures their potential dates are taking or not taking. They may just save time and energy on superfluous dating games.

Love seems to be much more needed and readily given in the time of Coronavirus – and the need for love is universal and everlasting. We witness the public love of healthcare workers and front-line essential workers, as well as outpouring of emails, texts, message, social media posts, virtual calls, and telephone conversations people share with their loved ones. The urge to connect substantiates a human belief in the common good and a sense of shared destiny. People have come together in isolation and find ways to share their deepest sorrow, grief, loss, or feelings of blissfulness about what one can still attain in the time of extremity.

The title of this article, *Love in the Time of Coronavirus*, echoes the power of love depicted in Gabriel Garcia Marquez's *Love in the Time of Cholera.* In the Covid-19 era, we can further attest that love, in its many forms, is the most viable foundation that can bring about necessary change to better our world while bringing us together as a whole. With love, we may begin to redirect anxiety and woe to mitigation, preparation, and remedy. With love, we may just come out of this disaster unscathed, stronger, better, and more conscious of what lies ahead for the world.

In the Covid-19 era, we can further attest that love, in its many forms, is the most viable foundation that can bring about necessary change to better our world while bringing us together as a whole.

(Originally published on https://aacs.website/wp-content/uploads/2021/07/AACSNL7.8.21.pdf)

23. Education in the Time of Coronavirus

According to a study from the United Nations, the COVID-19 pandemic has caused the largest disruption of education in history, "affecting nearly 1.6 billion learners in more than 190 countries and all continents. Closures of schools and other learning spaces have impacted 94 per cent of the world's student population, up to 99 per cent in low and lower-middle income countries." Along with the disruption, education disparities were exacerbated as vulnerable or underserved student populations were unable to adapt to distance learning effectively and/or a timely fashion. Gaps in student learning due to the unequal distribution of educational resources have widened. To say the least, education has changed forever in the time of Coronavirus. With the rise of online learning and digital platforms, educational key issues remain in inequality of resource distribution, access, as well as unfulfilled student needs for learning-style based differentiated education.

As the sudden, rapid, massive, and necessary movement of e-learning was enforced, many learners suffered from adaptation difficulties and insufficient bandwidth or technology, especially those with disadvantaged backgrounds. The digital divide was plain for all to see. Learning styles or differentiation needs of students also became an area of concern. For those who were more independent and had access to technology and educational resources, online learning could be more effective in terms of information retention: "students retain 25-60% more material when learning online compared to only 8-10% in a classroom." However, students who preferred proximity or hands-on learning could suffer from frustrations of technology management or navigation of course materials that appeared inexplicable or confusing to them.

The effectiveness of online learning varied among different age groups and learners. Younger children required more of a structured environment. Learners who were not technology oriented experienced difficulties and could lose interest altogether. Education in the time of Coronavirus, for many, was a lost cause. It was distressing and unmanageable for many students and families.

A pivot is underway; the real opportunity to reshape education cannot be overlooked.

For a post-pandemic education, it is crucial to make learning fun and effective through creative applications of technology; it is equally important to address different learning styles and provide differentiated online or offline instruction. More than a year after the lockdown, schools are beginning to reopen and are expected to operate in full swing in the 2021-2022 school year. Can the $1.9 trillion stimulus bill and its allotment bring back the normalcy education needs to provide for our young? Can we pick up where we left off and continue to strive for equitable learning opportunities for all? Can we -- students, teachers, parents, community leaders, politicians, be resilient and persistent enough to bridge the emotional, mental, economic, and academic gaps that Coronavirus imposed on us? In other words, can we take on the challenge of returning to normalcy but subverting the educational status-quo? A pivot is underway; the real opportunity to reshape education cannot be overlooked.

24. Digital Communications in the Time of Coronavirus

With social distancing measures in place to battle Covid-19, the world faces new challenges when trying to stay connected digitally. Increased use of social media, messaging apps, video conferencing programs, online entertainment, digital media or news, and internet resources is evident. People rely, more than ever, on digital platforms to shop for groceries and anything beyond daily necessities. Important and daunting questions remain as the world tries to grasp new realities in digital endeavors: Is the digital inequalities or gap widening or reducing? Are digital communications fair and trustworthy? What regulations or cautions should be raised for the digital world to function better or carry us forward?

The ubiquity of digital socialization and communications calls for thorough research on regulatory aspects of digital media use, including their ramifications for politics, journalism, public services, entertainment, gaming, e-commerce, education, healthcare, science or medical communication, and other areas.

Examining the scenarios in the U.S. alone, one can easily discern that a digital divide existed before Covid-19 hit. Pew Research shows that 25% of the U.S. population does not have broadband Internet access at home, and almost 20% does not use a smartphone. Other than the economic disparity, digital literacy issues can also be identified between people who use little messaging, voice, and videoconferencing, and those who are technology savvy.

The ubiquity of digital socialization and communications calls for thorough research on regulatory aspects of digital media use, including their ramifications for politics, journalism, public services, entertainment, gaming, e-commerce, education, healthcare, science or medical communication, and other areas. We have witnessed how detrimental it is to undergo an "infodemic" that misinforms the public, causes confusion, harm aspects of human life, and undermines credibility of our democratic systems. We need to educate the public about what sources of digital information to trust or avoid, how to evaluate claims and opinions, and how to stay critical and think from well-rounded and healthy perspectives to understand what is happening around the world. We must raise awareness about digital literacy through policies and mechanisms that come from not only the governments, but digital corporations and technology companies. Collaboration and coordination can create a digital world that portrays life from objective standpoints and delivers possibilities in a fair, just, and efficient fashion.

25. Things to Do in the Time of Coronavirus

Believe it or not, people still have fun doing all kinds of things in the time of Coronavirus. Outdoor activities have more appeals because open air is believed to dilute virus particles. Indoors, on the other hand, also provides fun engagements if one knows how to stay safe and vigilant. Those who are fully vaccinated can return to many indoor and outdoor activities without risks of getting infected and falling seriously ill.

Mayo Clinic and many blog sites list outdoor activities to do in the time of Coronavirus, and they are not very different from ordinary times:

- Walking, Running, and Hiking;
- Rollerblading and Biking;
- Fishing and Hunting;
- Golfing;
- Planting a Garden;
- Rock or Ice Climbing;

- Kayaking, Canoeing, Diving, Boating or Sailing;
- Skiing;
- Ice Skating;
- Snowboarding;
- Sledding;
- Snowshoeing;
- Fitness Classes;
- Picnics;
- Farmers Markets;
- Drive-in Movies;
- Restaurant Patio Dining;
- Camping;
- Swimming Pools and Beaches; (Water itself doesn't spread the COVID-19 virus.)
- Barbecues, Campfires and Outdoor Potlucks; and
- Sports/Sporting Events.

For indoors, the list goes on:

- Writing to Family and Friends;
- Writing;
- Watching Movies;

- Watching TV Shows;
- Learning New Skills;
- Learning New Instruments;
- Learn New Languages;
- Reading;
- Meditating;
- Caring for Your Health;
- Beautifying Yourself;
- Sort through Household Items;
- Arts and Craft;
- Board Games;
- Video Games;
- Indoor Exercise and Dance;
- Cooking;
- Baking;
- Foods and Drinks;
- Listening to Music;
- Knitting or Crocheting;
- Decorating'
- Chatting (Virtually or Not);
- Renovation Projects;
- Sing-alongs;

- Sleeping, Resting and Relax; and
- Planning for the Future.

Although we can't quite call the pandemic over yet, we must still live life to the fullest, make the best of any situation that exists, and embrace what is readily available to enjoy every single day. Keep in mind that mitigation measures are in place for our safety. Exercise caution in any activity or routine pursuit. Stay on the safe side and stay productive.

People still have fun doing all kinds of things in the time of Coronavirus.

26. Defying Cyberattacks in the Time of Coronavirus

The time of Coronavirus brings about not only increase use of technology, but also an explosion of cybersecurity incidents. Govtech reports on the concerning magnitude of cyberattacks:

- ***Bizjournals.com***: "Cyberattacks on the rise during the Covid-19 pandemic"
- ***Government Technology***: "How Is Covid-19 Creating Data Breaches?"
- ***BBC***: "Coronavirus: How the world of work may change forever"
- ***Interpol.int***: "INTERPOL report shows alarming rate of cyberattacks during COVID-19"
- ***Techxplore.com***: "Ransomware surge imperils hospitals as pandemic intensifies"

- ***PR Newswire***: "Top Cyber Security Experts Report: 4,000 Cyber Attacks a Day Since COVID-19 Pandemic"
- ***ZDNet***: "COVID-19 pandemic delivers extraordinary array of cybersecurity challenges"
- ***Maritime Executive***: "Maritime Cyberattacks Up by 400 Percent"

Most prominent is Evil Corp, a Russian cybercrime syndicate., which installs Ransomware in hundreds of US major companies, crippling healthcare, finance, oil supply and even governmental institutions:

- CNA Financial Paid Evil Hackers $40 Million in Ransom
- St. Joseph's Candler Ransomware Attack
- JBS Cyberattack

It becomes imperative that the public receives information and education during this time to defy the malicious attacks.

we can always start with ourselves to practice safe digital behavior.

From data breaches to ransomware and from online fraudulent activities to election security, new challenges call for necessary preventive measures on every level. First, know what you need to prevent; know that there are four kinds of attacks:

- Network Security Attacks
- Wireless Security Attacks
- Malware Attacks

- Social Engineering Attacks

However complicated and sophisticated cyberattacks may be, we can always start with ourselves to practice safe digital behavior.

- Safeguard and secure information -- Back up files.
- Double-check website safety – Enter only secure webpages.
- Keep your software and systems updated.
- Delete spam.
- Disable third-party components to prevent infiltration.
- Browse/click on only trusted webpages/links.
- Perform regular scans and cleaning.
- Use Domain-Based Message Authentication, Reporting and Conformance (DMARC).
- Use multi-factor authentication (MFA).

From individuals, communities, companies, to governments, we need to work together to raise awareness about cybersecurity. Organizations need to do the following:

- **Developing cyber security policies**

- **Implementing security awareness training**
- **Installing spam filters and anti-malware software**
- **Deploying Next-Generation Firewalls (NGFW)**
- **Installing endpoint detection & response (EDR)**

Whatever we do, however we work, stay vigilant. And hopefully with efforts from all sides, we can begin to defy cyberattacks in the time of coronavirus.

27. Lessons from the Time of Coronavirus

The past couple of years have been nothing short of disastraous and trying. We have encountered crisis after crisis. The Coronavirus pandemic, plenty of political and social tumoil, and an economic challenge like never before. However, crisis begets opportunity for personal growth, collective imporvement, and global alertness. In many ways, the time of Coronavirus is a time to learn and change for the better.

On a personal level, we learn many lessons about what our real priorities are in life. People we hold dear play important roles during this period. Their support carries us through difficult times and alleviates pain or agony that comes from loss of lives, lack of social interactions, and regular daily routines. We learn that health is the most important thing in life. Rich or poor, we are confronted with the same threat of a global pandemic that forces us to take a closer look at our diets, exercise habits, or lifestyles.

We learn to take care of our finances and be prepared for rainy days. We learn to work/educate ourselves differently and rely on technology to continue sharing and caring as a community. We are swamped with many changes, but we survive the worst situations and are ready to restore our world.

On a societal level, we learn to act and react fast. We learn to trust science, not misinformation from fear-mongers or reality-fabricators. We learn to stay productive after a period of forced hiatus. Our dormancy does not stop us from befriending technology or the digital world. We learn to gather and interact with mitigation measures and still accomplish our goals. We embrace the natural world and refuse to be completely isolated or let loneliness take over. We realize the urgency of certain issues that require global attention or cooperation: wealth or racial inequalities, environmental issues, crisis-response protocols, scientific research investments, and leaderships that work to sustain humanity and progress.

Our strength lies in the humanity or love that needs to be shared: the learnings and findings about human lives, about the human world, and about what paths we should rethink and take for the future.

"Humanity's memory is short, and what is not ever present fades quickly," Manisha Juthani, a Yale Medicine infectious diseases specialist, observes. The bubonic plague, ravaged Europe in the Middle Ages, and various viruses resurface again and again to threaten human lives. It is crucial to remember and learn from human history and experience. The time of coronavirus gives us a wake-up call; we cannot afford to return to the old normal but must "build back better" as the current US President proposes. We must keep in mind that next time, we may not be so lucky as to have multiple vaccines that can be distributed relatively efficiently. Think of the people or the regions of the world that still need to have equal access to the disease-fighting resources. We must recognize that we cannot win the battle and defeat the pandemic all by ourselves. Our strength lies in the humanity or love that needs to be shared: the learnings and findings about human lives, about the human world, and about what paths we should rethink and take for the future. Only with common goals and efforts, can we truly overcome crises and take opportunities to build a better world.

28. Democracy in the Time of Coronavirus

In the time of Coronavirus, many people question the principles of democracy because freedom seems to be "infringed upon" in many ways: people, a one point or for a period of time, must stay home, control gatherings, wear masks, practice social-distancing, and follow restricted travel guidelines. The ways of life are indeed, affected. However, it is too hasty for anyone to ascertain that democracy is hindered and people have lost their freedom. In a democracy, the wellfare of the public shall always be the top prority; it is up to a coutry to rally or react and optimize crisis-response outcomes -- at times, certain sacrifices are expected and inevitable. While a problematic government may use the pandemic as a ploy to oppress its civilians or manipulate information, a true leader can always abide by democratic principle to best work for his people's wellbeing and benefit.

Many countries showed a leadership debacle where violence or abuse of power resulted from lockdowns and pandemic mitigation measures manifesting itself through politicization and ideological propaganda. Freedom House researches the impact of COVID-19 on democracy and human rights. Based on a study on 192 countries, it proposes that "the COVID-19 pandemic is exacerbating the 14 years of consecutive decline in freedom.... The findings illustrate the breadth and depth of the assault on democracy." Taking a closer look at home -- America, the world's leading democracy, under the previous administration, it declines in its international standing due to dubious narratives and false information about the pandemic. Under the current administration, we start to see the light at the end of the tunnel and things are trending in the right direction. Democracy is intact: it can deliver for people under the current government.

While a problematic government may use the pandemic as a ploy to oppress its civilians or manipulate information, a true leader can always abide by democratic principle to best work for his people's wellbeing and benefit.

Interesting enough, whether the time of Coronavirus is spent in campaigns of tyrannical threats, harassment, or manipulation has very little to do with a country's political system. While authoritarians are quick to restrict individual freedoms, they are not the only ones during this time to make tough choices and decisions. Can democracy, then, survive the time of Coronavirus and deliver for its people what it is designed to do:

liberty and justice for all – a country of the people, by the people, and for the people? Premature speculations on the future of democracy abounds. However, all the evidence of infringement upon democratic values does not necessarily decree failure or death of democracy. Rather, it portends how a leader can lose or win the battle with a virus, as well as how crucial it is to have a sanguine leadership to carry a country out of the shadow of this time. The lesson here is clear: one must rethink and always bear in mind the necessary checks and balances for the wellbeing of the public, no matter who is in power or what political philosophy is in favor.

29. Coming Together for Global Peace and Growth

In the process of examining world issues, one can discern that human conflict, inhumanity, climate change, and imbalance in allocation of resources construct the key factors that hinder world peace and growth. To tackle relevant challenges, the world needs to come together to make efforts for sustainable development and growth. Coming together implies that peoples are capable of viewing and positioning themselves as citizens of one global community.

The notion of a global community is of a vision affirmed by ancient seers, poets, and visionaries. The UN was formed after WWII in 1945, among many other world alliances and networks. Most notably, international humanitarian organizations, women's and youth movements, and individuals seeking to contribute and support world peace and growth have been emerging. Communication and information about the world as a community has become unprecedentedly efficient through advanced technology, news, and the internet.

The world is more interconnected than ever. However, world peace is still a work in process. Indeed, globalization of the economy benefits all, but the struggle among economic powers creates human conflict and severe inequality. People of all nations may proclaim their desire for world peace, but cooperation, collaboration, open and honest communication, and the redistribution of wealth, still leaves much to be desired.

How then, can the world come together? We could ban weapons of mass destruction, prohibit the sale of arms to waring countries and regions, coordinate and allocate resources, and squash crime/violation of human rights. We could not, however, deny peoples' basic instinct for self-preservation and self-interest. The key lies in each and every individual's ability to self-reflect, self-criticize, and stay self-reliant, which composes the root of global competence and global cooperation/ collaboration. Self-awareness, curiosity, and desire to learn and grow, is the intrinsic transformation one needs to come together with the whole world. Extreme or unbridled nationalism is, then, an obstacle to world peace and growth, to the love of humanity as a whole. One needs to learn to acquire a birds-eye view to identify and realize the blind spot to world peace and growth: fear of others has far-reaching implications of incapability to grow and move forward as a planet.

In other words, inequalities concerning race, gender, and social/economic class, are the ultimate barriers to world peace and growth. Learning/ embracing differences and celebrating universality can keep the world moving forward while maintaining legitimate pride in one's own country and culture. Transparency and accountability can lead to justice and prosperity. When more people(s) become globally competent, the world may advance from struggling to resolve conflict to improving people's lives in environments of their own choosing. In turn, true freedom and harmony many be achieved for all.

"Think Global Live Noble" -- together we can build a better world!

First Printed in <u>Global Competence Revisited</u> (2019)

30. Are We Prepared for the Next Pandemic?

More than a year ago on March 11, 2020, the World Health Organization declared Covid-19 a global pandemic. As we learn to grasp coping measures and treatments for this coronavirus, we are very aware that the crisis is not over, and other viruses will rise to threaten humanity again in the future. Are we prepared for the next disaster? Other than public health concerns and scientific/medical solutions, we realize that ineffective leadership or coordination within national and international governments can cause a ton of harm and damage. To get ready for any emergency, it is crucial to address inefficacy and reform crisis-response processes.

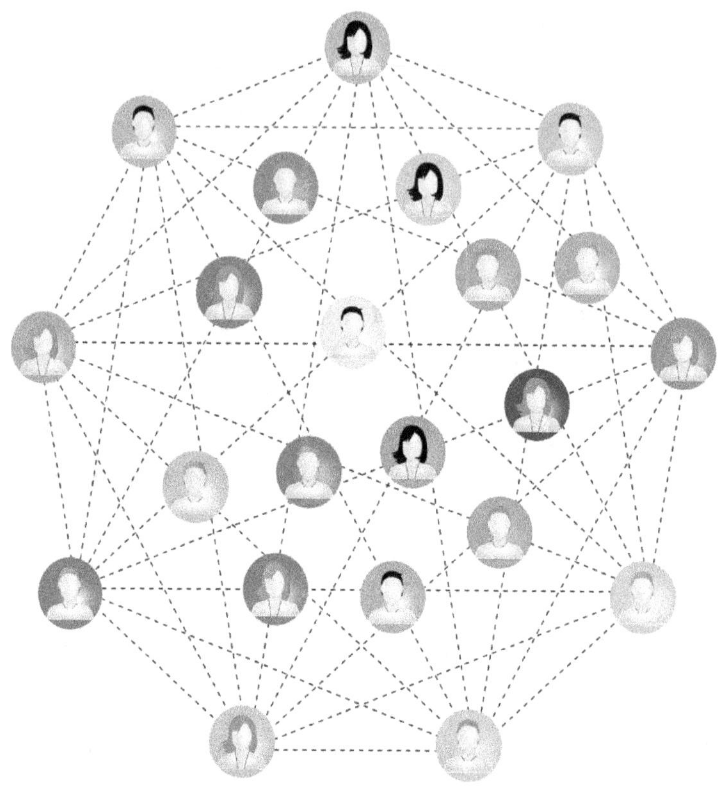

No country can survive and prosper without global collaboration, especially in a Pandemic. We need a better plan and to prepare for supplies, equipment, public awareness, equal access to resources. We can start fixing broken, profit-driven healthcare systems, educate our people, nurture responsible citizens who can think not only themselves, but for others.

Perhaps the most efficient way to prepare people for a calamity is to educate them about health, survival skills, household readiness, and staying informed/avoiding misinformation during ordinary times. Equally important is to conduct ongoing medical research and development and gain public trust and investment in these areas. On a personal level, people need to be financially, mentally, and logistically organized for unforeseen disruptions in life; on the societal level, partnerships need to be established to collaborate promptly on action items. Experts also suggest strategies to tackle the next pandemic: use systems in place to identify threats such as watch lists, response networks, and emergency management systems; inform, prepare, and guide the public; coordinate efforts among healthcare providers, governments, and families; streamline operations and control infrastructural/supply chains; and adapt to and build on the new normal.

War-time efforts are indeed required in the time of Coronavirus. The post-pandemic world needs continued endeavor to improve and renovate. No country can survive and prosper without global collaboration, especially in a Pandemic. We need a better plan and to prepare for supplies, equipment, public awareness, equal access to resources. We can start fixing broken, profit-driven healthcare systems, educate our people, nurture responsible citizens who can think not only themselves, but for others. Yes, we can be prepared -- we can do anything if we work together.

Appendix

The Benefit of Diversity

The immigration issue fuels emotions as we have seen both in the recent political discourse and in the world throughout history. Many politicians such as Donald J. Trump find that their poll numbers rise the further from reality they drift. Republicans are far more certain than Democrats (53 percent versus 24 percent) that immigration is making our society worse.

As Ted Widmer affirms in the New York Times (Oct. 6, 2015), history provides some clarity about the relative costs and benefits of immigration over time. Fifty years ago Lyndon B. Johnson signed the Immigration and Nationality Act of 1965 at the foot of the Statue of Liberty. It made the United States a stronger nation. What ensued was arguably the most significant period of immigration in American history. Nearly 59 million people have come to the United States since 1965, and three-quarters of them came from Latin America and Asia. The flood of new immigrants promoted prosperity in ways that few could have imagined in 1965. Between 1990 and 2005, as the digital age took off, 25 percent of the fastest-growing American companies were founded by people born in foreign countries.

The 2010 census stated that more than 50 percent of technical workers in Silicon Valley are Asian-American. Google was co-founded by Sergey Brin, who emigrated from the Soviet Union with his parents at age 6. The C.E.O. of United Airlines is Mexican-American. And an extraordinary number of Indian-Americans have risen to become chief executives of other major American corporations, including Adobe Systems, Pepsi, Motorola and Microsoft.

In countless other ways, we might measure the improvements since 1965. A prominent AIDS researcher, David Ho, came to this country as a 12-year-old from Taiwan. Immigrants helped take the space program to new places, and sometimes gave their lives in that cause (an Indian-American astronaut, Kalpana Chawla, perished in the Columbia space shuttle disaster). Furthermore, American culture, in all aspects of music, art, cuisine, and others, became more interesting as it grew more diverse. A careful consideration of the 1965 Immigration Act shows that America's willingness to lower barriers made it a better country.

Lyndon B. Johnson signed the Immigration and Nationality Act on Oct. 3, 1965.

The Immigration and Nationality Act made America a genuinely New Frontier, younger and more diverse, truer to its ideals. On the other hand, it certainly increased American security from a more conservative standpoint. Significant numbers of immigrants and their children joined the United States military after 1965, and the armed forces became more ethnically diverse.

(Originally published on: http://www.aacs.website/wp-content/uploads/2015/07/AACSNL11.111.pdf; first printed in Asia-Literacy and Global Competence, 2017)

Study Questions for *The Un-death of Me*

One reader has suggested that reading my book *The Un-death of Me* was an exercise to become globally competent. I appreciate this observation of the reader, and confirm that my debut book and this collection of articles in *Global Competence Revisited* have similar purposes of examining the issues concerning cultural diversity and competence. I therefore, include as an addendum here, study questions for *The Un-death of Me.* In doing so, I hope to circle back to address some of the subjects I explore and elicit further discussions.

Discussion Questions for The Un-death of Me:

1. Do you think this "fictional memoir" is more fictional or autobiographical? To what extent is this book a cross-genre endeavor?
2. Does the book start in a disoriented way with a purpose? What purpose does it serve? Reflect on Avery/the protagonist narrator's state of mind and how "stream of consciousness" brings out her stories.
3. What kind of character is Harry? When Avery says she needs to teach people how she is to be treated, including adults and children, do you think she has this man and her students/step kids in mind? What other characters might be included in this list of people that need to be taught about cultural competence?
4. Do you think the character of Avery Mingli Liang is well developed? How has she

changed throughout the book? What kind of realizations does she experience? To what extent is her isolation self-imposed? Does she establish true connections with her husband Abbey Lori? Or is it another quandary?

5. What kind of character is Tim Rosenberg? Abbey Lori? How are they similar or different? Why do you think these two men become the most important influencers on Avery's life?
6. Do you think you can be truly empathetic of Avery's immigration life and experience? Based on your own upbringing and heritage, can you picture what Avery has to undergo in order to find her niche in American society?
7. How sympathetic are you of people of foreign origins? Do you think they should all go home to avoid struggles in their adopted countries? Or, what do immigrant experiences like Avery's teach you?
8. What is your favorite part of the book? Why?

9. **The differences and similarities among nations are nuanced in this book. Compare and contrast. Give examples.**
10. **The prologue/epilogue of the book draws out the same topic of quest and life fulfilment. To what extent do you think the implications change although they both employs very much of the same narration?**

(First printed in Asia-Literacy and Global Competence, 2017)

Thank you for reading!

Dear Reader,

I hope you enjoyed the entries collected in *Writings in the Time of Coronavirus.* In foregrounding aspects life affected during the pandemic, I aim to raise awareness about cultural empathy and sensitivity. All human beings are on the same boat when it comes to a disaster that hits the entire world: rich or poor, every individual suffers and must adapt to the new order. In order to recover from the calamity and build a better world, one needs to learn from the experience, transform his or her share of life in the time of Coronavirus to contribute to a collective understanding of what the world can do better next time when a tragedy of similar magnitude occurs.

Global competence, again, is the key to world peace and growth. My journey of learning continues and will never cease. I plan to keep writing about different facets of our global community. Our complex yet beautiful world has so much to offer, that it's hard not to explore as many aspects as our time allows us to.

Finally, I need to ask a favor. If you are so inclined, I'd love a review of *Writings in the Time of Coronavirus*. Your honest review is the most precious feedback I could have.

You, the reader, have the power to make voices heard and change our world for the better. Please find below a link to my author page on Amazon:
http://amazon.com/author/aliciasulozeron

Other platforms where you could communicate your thoughts about my book are as follows:

http://www.aacs.website/en/membership/featured
https://www.facebook.com/people/Alicia-Lozeron/100013834032346
https://www.facebook.com/aliciasulozeron
http://www.aliciasulozeron.com/

Please make yourself heard by voicing your opinions. Thank you so much again for reading. I look forward to reading your review.

Sincerely,

Alicia Su Lozeron

Writings in the Time of Coronavirus

Author: Alicia Su Lozeron

About the Author

Global Competence Mentor | Author | Licensed Secondary-School English Language Arts and Chinese Mandarin Teacher |

Think Global Live Noble

Alicia Su Lozeron is the author of numerous news/magazine articles, short stories, and novels. She holds a Master's degree in English and Comparative Literature from Columbia University in the City of New York, is licensed as a secondary-school English Language Arts/Chinese Mandarin teacher in the U.S, and served as a college English adjunct instructor. Through her writing career, she aims to raises awareness about global competence, and to connect the world through global explorations and studies. Asia-literacy and Global Competence (2017), Global Competence Revisited (2019), and Writings in the Time of Coronavirus (2021), collections of her articles and vignettes, highlight her musings of cultural interactions and layouts the groundwork for her many endeavors. (See both English and Chinese versions at https://www.amazon.com/Alicia-Su-Lozeron/e/B01N3LXBAN).

Her debut novel, The Un-death of Me, depicts a world traveler and immigrant Asian American woman's life in a fresh light. It is a fictional world full of contemporary and global resonance; it is about many subjects: alienation, individuality, self-doubt, self-discovery, complexities of love and marriage, quests of fulfillment and happiness, (in)justice, cultural diversity, discrimination, and mankind as a whole. Its subtle yet intense emotions detailed in the many characters and locales, render a visionary sense of humanity, gratifying and unforgettable in their own rights. (See https://www.amazon.com/Un-death-Me-Asian-American-Woman/dp/0998194123/ref=asap_bc?ie=UTF8).

Alicia Su Lozeron
Publisher: Asia-America Connection Society
Think Global Live Noble
Phone 702-505-9506
E-mail aliciasulozeron@gmail.com; info@aacs.website

Below is what readers and audiences have discerned of Alicia Su Lozeron's work:

• helps me overcome difficulties or fears and find beauty in positive human interactions;
• helps me appreciate people of various backgrounds, and expand knowledge about the world;
• helps me understand interracial or blended family relations;
• helps me savor intricate feelings and emotions about important subjects in life;
• helps me gain enjoyment through poetic narrations;
• helps me realize a new perspective of hope, courage, and respect for others;
• helps me raise awareness about cultural competence;
• helps me nurture a well-rounded global outlook;
• motivates me to promote an open/just community;

• urges me to develop the ability to see the big picture using multiple frames of references;
• helps me strengthen the ability to express genuine love;
• helps me decrease conflict by learning to trust and to resolve disagreements….

"Think Global Live Noble" -- together we can build a better world!

Detailed Information:
https://www.linkedin.com/in/alicia-su-lozeron
http://www.aliciasulozeron.com
http://amazon.com/author/aliciasulozeron
http://www.aacs.website/en/services/authors-and-books
https://www.facebook.com/aliciasulozeron
https://www.facebook.com/people/Alicia-Lozeron/100013834032346
http://www.aacs.website
https://www.facebook.com/aacs.website
https://twitter.com/AliciaSuLozeron

www.ingramcontent.com/pod-product-compliance
Lightning Source LLC
Chambersburg PA
CBHW081127300726

48982CB00005B/875
* 9 7 8 1 7 3 3 2 0 3 9 3 7 *